VOLCANOES

Shirley Duke

rourkeeducationalmedia.com

Before Reading:

Building Academic Vocabulary and Background Knowledge

Before reading a book, it is important to tap into what your child or students already know about the topic. This will help them develop their vocabulary, increase their reading comprehension, and make connections across the curriculum.

1. *Look at the cover of the book. What will this book be about?*
2. *What do you already know about the topic?*
3. *Let's study the Table of Contents. What will you learn about in the book's chapters?*
4. *What would you like to learn about this topic? Do you think you might learn about it from this book? Why or why not?*
5. *Use a reading journal to write about your knowledge of this topic. Record what you already know about the topic and what you hope to learn about the topic.*
6. *Read the book.*
7. *In your reading journal, record what you learned about the topic and your response to the book.*
8. *After reading the book complete the activities below.*

Content Area Vocabulary
Read the list. What do these words mean?

basalt
caldera
convection
lahars
magma
molten
pyroclastic
rifts
subduction
tectonic
vents
volcanologist

After Reading:

Comprehension and Extension Activity

After reading the book, work on the following questions with your child or students in order to check their level of reading comprehension and content mastery.

1. *Why do people live near volcanoes? (Summarize)*
2. *In what ways are earthquakes and tsunamis connected to volcanoes? (Infer)*
3. *Have you ever been to a volcano or near a volcano such as Yellowstone or in Hawaii? What was the land surrounding these volcanoes like? (Text to self connection)*
4. *Which do you think is more deadly: the volcano eruption or the aftermath of the eruption? Explain. (Asking questions)*
5. *Explain the differences between caldera and strato volcanoes. (Summarize)*

Extension Activity

Yellowstone is considered a supervolcano. What are supervolcanoes? Where are they located? Research supervolcanoes and find out what makes them different from the volcanoes you read about. Create a poster, brochure, or other presentation explaining supervolcanoes and how to be prepared in case you encounter one!

TABLE OF CONTENTS

WHAT IS A VOLCANO?

Volcanoes begin deep within the Earth. Hot, **molten** rock called **magma** collects far underground. Forces below it crack the underground rock. Pressure pushes melted rock upward through these openings. The molten rock explodes from the opening or flows out.

The molten rock is now lava. Once cooled, the lava solidifies and becomes igneous rock. Over time, a cone shape builds up.

Hot Fact
Igneous rock is one of three main types of rocks. The other types are sedimentary and metamorphic.

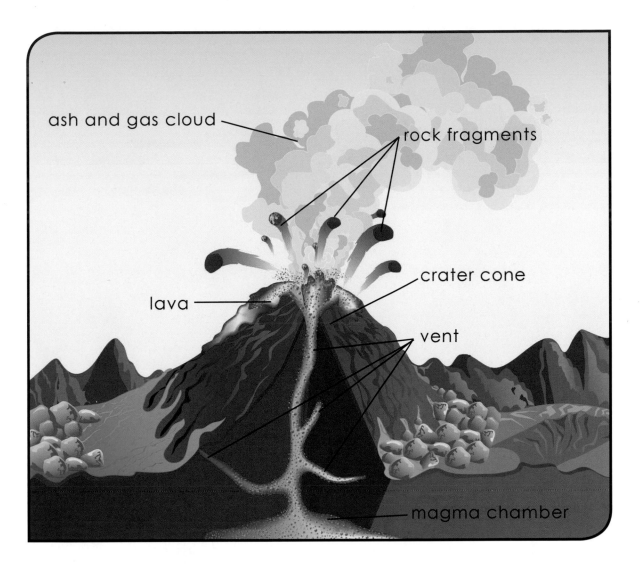

ash and gas cloud

rock fragments

crater cone

lava

vent

magma chamber

Magma chambers underground hold different amounts of magma. Cracks and **vents** allow the hot magma to move upward and collect in chambers in volcanoes. Certain conditions force the magma above ground, where it cools as lava.

Did You Know?

The word volcano came from the name of the Roman god Vulcan. People once thought the lava and gas clouds erupting from the island of Vulcano was Vulcan forging thunderbolts for Jupiter, king of their gods, and for Mars, their god of war.

Mt. Kilimanjaro in Tanzania is a dormant volcano. It is the tallest mountain in Africa and is 19,341 feet (5,895 meters) tall.

Volcanoes that have produced lava or eruptions in the past 10,000 years, or since the Ice Age, are active volcanoes. Eruptions happen when molten rock, gases, and ash from below the Earth's surface are forced up and out through cracks.

Hot Fact
Alaska contains three-fourths of the volcanoes that have erupted in the past 200 years.

Dormant volcanoes are active volcanoes that are not erupting, but are expected to erupt again. Extinct volcanoes have not erupted in at least 10,000 years and are not expected to erupt again. Still, some extinct volcanoes have surprised people and erupted in the past.

Types of Volcanoes

Volcanoes are often classified by shape and how they were formed. However, not every kind of eruption falls into a single group. The speed of the flowing lava builds the shape.

Slow-moving lava forms a gently sloping cone called shield volcanoes. They are not normally explosive. Shield volcanoes are most often **basalt,** a type of lava that is very liquid and flows easily.

This view of Mauna Loa from Mauna Kea in the late evening shows the distinctive shape of shield volcanoes.

Mauna Loa, one of five volcanoes that form the island of Hawaii, is one of the largest active volcanoes today. The mountain it forms is 60 miles (97 kilometers) long and 30 miles (48 kilometers) wide. Mauna Loa is the Hawaiian term for long mountain. It is a shield volcano. Its eruptions have averaged one every six years for the past 300 years.

Cinder cones are the simplest type of volcanoes. Lava flows out of a central vent and down the sides, forming a cone.

The lava in a cinder cone volcano cools quickly. It builds up rock to form the typical steep-sided cone. The cinder cone can be part of another volcano system, such as one growing on a shield volcano. Paricutin in Mexico is a cinder cone volcano.

Strato volcanoes produce two types of lavas. These lavas are thicker and cooler than basalt. The thick lavas often plug the opening. Different gases build up below the plug. They make a more explosive eruption when they blow. The tall sides may trigger mud or landslides and earthquakes during an eruption.

The lava pours down the volcano's sides. Cooled layers of rock form the sides. Strato volcanoes are also called composite volcanoes. Over half of the world's volcanoes are strato volcanoes. Mt. St. Helens, Mt. Rainier, and Mt. Fuji are strato volcanoes.

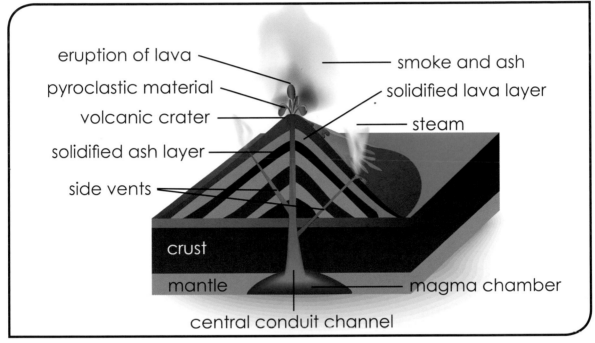

Magma comes from the upper, fluid part of the mantle and moves upward and out through a variety of vents.

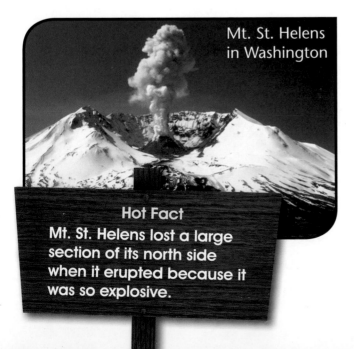

Mt. St. Helens in Washington

Hot Fact
Mt. St. Helens lost a large section of its north side when it erupted because it was so explosive.

Mt. Rainier in Washington

Mt. Fuji in Japan

Geothermal features such as hot springs get their colors from pigmented bacteria called thermophiles, which means heat-loving.

Caldera volcanoes form when the whole top of the volcano blows off from an explosion. These volcanoes usually have large magma chambers. Their eruptions can cause the mountain to collapse into itself. The giant opening left is a caldera. These immense eruptions spread ash over hundreds of miles. The Yellowstone area is an example of a caldera volcano.

A lava field is a large area of almost flat lava flows.

Lava comes from the Earth in other ways as well. A collection of vents and openings together may not form a typical volcano but lava flows from them. These separate eruptions spread over the area. They don't usually have large amounts of magma.

The Columbia River Basalt Group stretches across Washington, Oregon, Idaho, Nevada, and California. Etched and shaped by Ice Age floods, it is one of the best-preserved continental flood basalt provinces on Earth.

Flood basalts aren't typical volcanoes, either. These slowly moving lava fields may grow deep and cover large areas of land. The Columbia River basin in Washington is an example of flood basalts.

Lava also comes from mid-ocean ridges, where the Earth's forces spread apart the ocean's floor. The lava flows in and fills the opening—all underwater.

This molten rock called magma comes from deep below the Earth's surface. Its molten form is a result of forces within the Earth and its layers.

Magma can reach temperatures of 1,300 degrees Fahrenheit (700 degrees Celsius) to 2,400 degrees Fahrenheit (1,300 degrees Celsius).

VOLCANO FORMATION

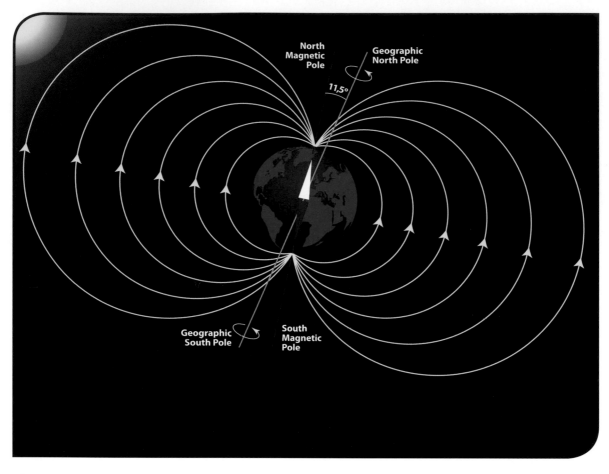

The iron moving on convection currents in the core creates the magnetic field around the Earth.

The forces that shape volcanoes begin inside the Earth's layers. The inside layer is the core. It is formed of two parts—the inner and outer core. The inner core is mostly iron, with some nickel. The pressure is so great that the metals compress into solids.

The outer core is made of iron and nickel. This part of the core is in motion. This moving metal makes the Earth's magnetic field.

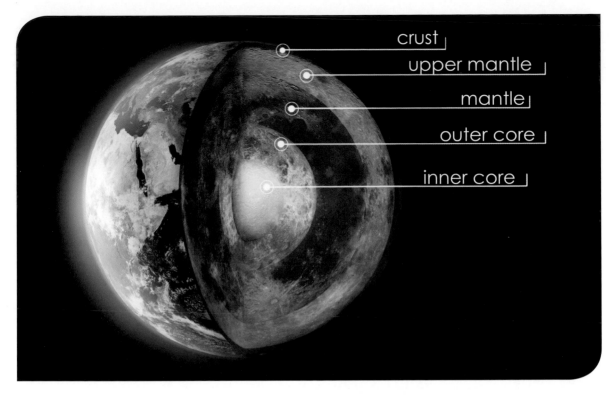

The Earth's hot core heats the mantle, causing it to move toward the surface and spread apart. This motion causes it to thicken and cool somewhat.

The middle layer, or mantle, is a combination of solid and liquid rock. The lower mantle is solid rock, which is hot enough to melt.

This layer stays solid because of the great pressure at that depth. The upper mantle's lower section is both rock and molten rock. The upper part is thicker and firmer because it's cooler.

The outside layer is the crust. The crust is the thinnest layer. The continental crust ranges in thickness from five miles to 44 miles (eight kilometers to 70 kilometers). It is made of mostly granite and other rocks. The ocean crust is under the ocean water. It's about five miles (eight kilometers) thick. Ocean crust is formed of basalt, another type of rock.

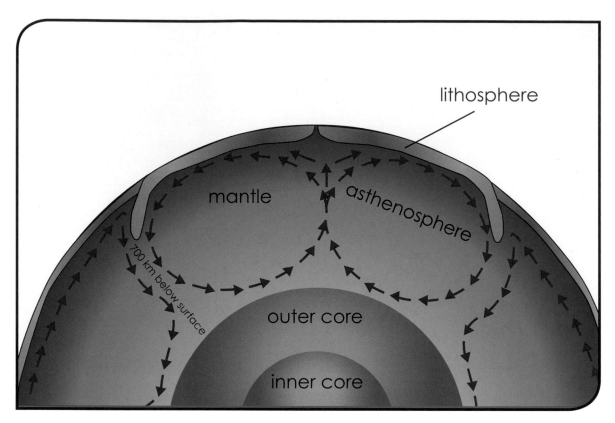

Convection currents cause the magma to move because the heated liquid rock rises and then as it cools, it falls. Convection currents are the driving force for the motion of the Earth's tectonic plates.

The Earth's crust isn't a continuous slab of solid rock. It is in sections called **tectonic** plates. They move slowly above the mantle on **convection** currents caused by the heat inside the Earth. The motion causes cracks in the crust called faults. The hot magma moves up in the cracks and finally erupts.

Tectonic plates crash together and pull apart. As the plates move apart, **rifts** are formed. The underlying magma moves in to fill in the rift, creating new rock. Plates moving together collide at the **subduction** zone. Heavier ocean crust sliding into the lighter continental crust dives under the continental crust. This shifting causes vibrations called earthquakes and creates volcanoes.

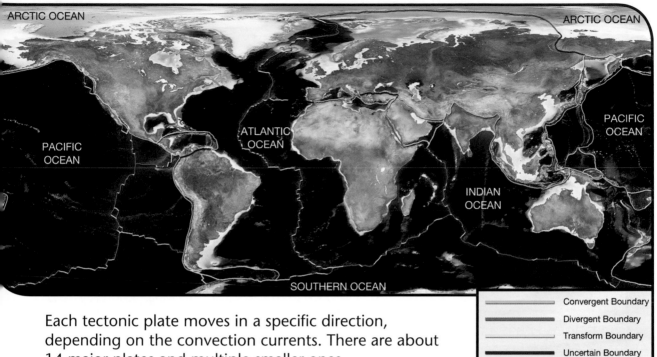

Each tectonic plate moves in a specific direction, depending on the convection currents. There are about 14 major plates and multiple smaller ones.

	Convergent Boundary
	Divergent Boundary
	Transform Boundary
	Uncertain Boundary

Millions of years ago, the Earth was a single mass of land called Pangea. The plates slowly drifted apart, forming today's continents. Notice how South America's outline fits into Africa's shape.

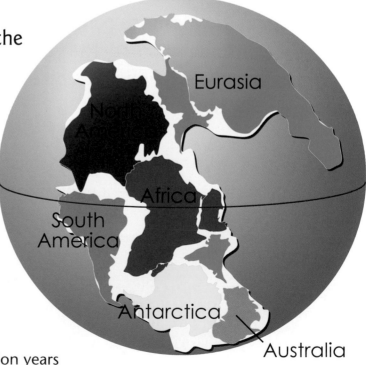

Pangea formed about 300 million years ago. It began to break up after about 100 million years.

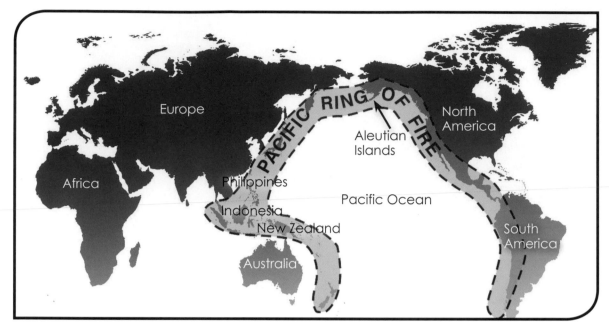

The Ring of Fire is a ring of volcanoes and earthquake zones around the Pacific Ocean. About 90 percent of all earthquakes are found along the Ring of Fire and 75 percent of all volcanoes are located there.

Volcanoes form around the plate boundaries. The best known region of volcanoes comes from the Pacific plate moving under the continental crust. The collisions cause cracks that allow magma to swell upward. Colliding plates form the most explosive volcanoes.

The loop of volcanoes around the Pacific Ocean is called the Ring of Fire. Countries anywhere along this region can be affected.

Did You Know?
Hawaii has three active volcanoes. Maunaloa last erupted in 1984 and Kilauea has been erupting since 1983. The third volcano, Loihi, is an undersea mountain off the coast of the state's Big Island.

Kilauea volcano lava

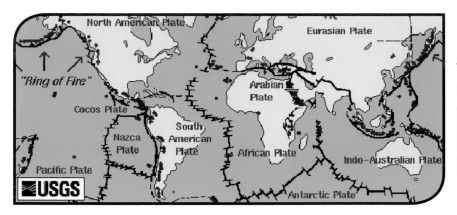

This world map shows the location of volcanoes. Note how many are located at plate boundaries.

Volcanoes erupt around the world. They can develop anywhere tectonic plates meet and subduct. Subduction occurs when one plate moves under another and sinks into the Earth's mantle.

Other regions have spreading plates. The spreading plates also form volcanoes. Iceland, the Kenya Rift Valley, Italy, and Hawaii all have active volcanoes from rifts.

Mt. Longonot is a crater volcano in the Great Rift Valley of Kenya. The crater is about one mile (1.6 kilometers) across. It has been dormant since 1863.

Volcanic hot spots form over a plume of magma below ground. The small, fixed source of magma pushes upward as the tectonic plates move over it and melts the crust above it. This often results in chains of islands. The Hawaiian Islands were formed this way.

The Hawaiian Islands were formed as the Pacific plate moved over a hot spot, which remained stationary. The islands to the northwest are the oldest.

Volcano eruptions are fascinating and even frightening at times. Their impact is felt in multiple ways.

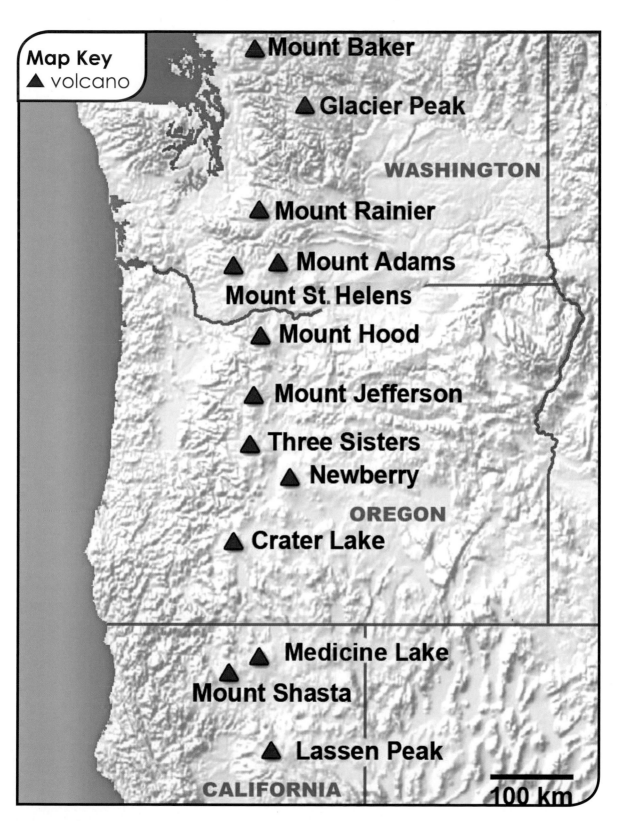

▲ Mount Baker

▲ Glacier Peak

WASHINGTON

▲ Mount Rainier

▲   ▲ Mount Adams
Mount St. Helens

▲ Mount Hood

▲ Mount Jefferson

▲ Three Sisters
▲ Newberry

OREGON

▲ Crater Lake

▲ Medicine Lake
▲
Mount Shasta

▲ Lassen Peak

CALIFORNIA

100 km

Cascades, a mountain range in the continental Unites States, holds a large number of active volcanoes. Seven of them have been active in the past 300 years. Mt. St. Helens is the best-studied volcano, following its huge eruption in 1980.

EFFECTS OF VOLCANOES

Volcanic eruptions can have minor effects. Others may affect countless people and large areas. About 500 volcanoes are active around the world.

Between 10 and 40 volcanoes erupt every year. They affect the climate and environment, peoples' health, and the economy. Other effects include **pyroclastic** flows, mudslides, toxic gases, earthquakes, and tsunamis.

An eruption magnitude scale tells the size of a volcanic explosion. The rating scale is the Volcanic Explosivity Index, or VEI. It is based on many of the events taking place during an eruption. A Hawaiian volcano rating is low because it's not explosive. A Strombolian rating means a low-erupting force volcano. The lava shooting out from a central crater is liquid basalt lava.

Mount Etna is Europe's highest and most active volcano. It is located above the city of Catania on the island of Sicily.

VEI	Plume Height	Classification	Frequency of Eruption	Example
0	< 100 m	Hawaiian	Persistent	Kilauea
1	100-1000 m	Haw/ Strombolian	Daily	Stromboli
2	1-5 km	Strom/Vulcanian	Weekly	Galeras, 1992
3	3-15 km	Vulcanian	Few months	Ruiz,1985
4	10-25 km	Vulc/Plinian	≥ 1 yr	Galunggung, 1982
5	>25 km	Plinian	≥ 10 yrs	St. Helens, 1980
6	>25 km	Plin/Ultra-Plinian	≥ 100 yrs	Krakatau, 1883
7	>25 km	Ultra-Plinian	≥ 1,000 yrs	Tambora, 1815
8	>25 km	Ultra-Plinian	≥ 10,000 yrs	Yellowstone, 2 Ma

A Vulcanian rating means the eruption increases in intensity. It has explosive force and sends out burning, thick lava in chunks. A Plinian level is explosive. It sends out a steady

Volcanic ash is hard, sharp, and doesn't dissolve in water. It covers everything in its path.

stream of chunky magma and gases at high speeds. Tall columns of erupting material are visible.

Ash is one of the earliest effects of an eruption. It spreads through the air and covers homes, fields, roads, and buildings. It affects air quality and irritates eyes and skin. Ash weight may collapse roofs. Large explosions often kill people outright. They produce so much ash that many people die from crop loss and famine. Falling rocks and pumice, or foamy air-filled lava, rain down below.

Most lava flows move slowly, so it's possible to get away from them. However, pyroclastic flows can move between 161 and 322 miles per hour (259 to 322 kilometers per hour). You can't outrun those speeds.

Volcanoes release various gases, which spread out in the air. The biggest danger from gases comes from near the vent. Continual eruptions can cause long-term breathing problems.

Aircraft cannot safely fly through ash clouds. Ash is formed of tiny glass particles and minerals. Aircraft engines melt the ash that goes into them. The melted ash is forced into all engine parts and then solidifies, causing engines to stall.

Hot Fact
The Eyjafjallajökull explosion in Iceland in 2010 shut down air traffic for weeks. It affected the airlines and passengers, costing billions of dollars in losses.

Lava and ash can engulf cities and towns. Heavy ash changes climates, hurts water supplies and waste disposal, and destroys surrounding plants and trees.

A violent eruption in Chaiten, Chile, in 2008 covered the town in ash and mud flows.

Did You Know?

Mt. Vesuvius erupted near Naples, Italy, in 79 CE. Tons of falling debris covered Pompeii and two other towns. People were caught unaware and buried under the falling materials and ash. Their remains were not discovered until 1748. Excavations at the site are still underway today.

People were caught by surprise when Mt. Vesuvius erupted. Many were buried in the intense pyroclastic flow, which preserved their bodies in stone.

The upper layer of lava cools first and forms a thin crust of rock on top of the lava flow.

Lava covers the land, burning the area around it. It cools and hardens into rock. The rock remains for years. Volcanoes build and change the shape of the land. They form new rocks and improve the soil by adding minerals. They create new mountains and islands.

These changes happen far more quickly than changes by glaciers, wind, and water. The shape and makeup of the land is affected for years.

AFTER A VOLCANO

Millions of people live near volcanoes. The fertile soil around them brings people to the region. Others live there because they don't have the means to move elsewhere. Volcanoes can't be prevented. People living near them should be prepared for an eruption.

Explosions blast hot rocks, molten rock, and gas into the air. Ash flows occur along the volcano's sides. Wind carries the ash for hundreds of miles.

Gases and smoke coming from a volcano can signal a pending eruption.

Hot ash and lava melt ice and snow around the top of a volcano. The melted water mixes with ash, soil, and debris as it flows rapidly down the volcano's side. Heavy rain erodes these deposits to make mudflows, or **lahars**. They flood the valleys around the volcano.

Lahars flow down the mountain and enter waterways, such as this river. Layers of ash often land on top.

Flash floods, hot ash flow, and fires from the heat can erupt. Rockfalls, earthquakes, and tsunamis may be triggered by an eruption. Many people are killed by the events after a volcano.

Did You Know?
David A. Johnston, a 30-year-old **volcanologist**, was studying volcanic gas studies at Mount St. Helens on May 18, 1980. He believed being on-site gave more information and thought he was in a safe observation post. The Mount St. Helens eruption carried him away that day. His death convinced officials to keep the area around the volcano closed.

Lahars and material ejected from a volcanic explosion can suddenly bury buildings and roads.

Homes aren't safe during an eruption. Have a plan in place. Keep up with the news. Avoid low areas and follow evacuation directions if they are given.

After an eruption, move away from ash falls. Use masks and goggles to protect your lungs and eyes. Clear ash off the roofs of homes to prevent collapse. Don't drive while ash is falling because it clogs engines.

The eruption itself is dangerous, but much of the danger comes from the resulting floods, mudslides, downed power lines, and fires. Local police and firefighters arrive to direct traffic and care for the injured. Cities provide shelters if evacuations are needed.

Be Prepared
Keep emergency supplies on hand, including:
- flashlight and batteries
- first-aid supplies
- extra food and water
- manual can opener
- family medicines
- dust masks and goggles
- sturdy, closed-toe shoes

State health departments monitor the effects after an eruption. They work with the affected region to keep people healthy and informed of the dangers. Other organizations are called in as needed.

The Federal Emergency Response Agency (FEMA) may arrive to help. They bring needed supplies. The Red Cross organization works to provide immediate assistance to people who lost their homes or can't return to them.

Early warning signs of eruptions help government agencies prepare. They can set up a zone around the volcano to keep people away from danger. They determine evacuation plans and stock up on supplies that will be needed after an eruption. They secure money for aid and set up communication systems.

Volunteers from the Red Cross youth organization prepare for a volcano disaster by participating in a training simulation. The training allows them to practice responding to a real emergency.

Geologists who study volcanoes are **volcanologists**. They work to predict volcano eruptions before they happen. They arrive after an eruption to study the particular causes and effects. Learning about an eruption helps them predict future eruptions.

A scientist from the USGS Hawaiian Volcano Observatory evaluates gas emissions coming from Kilauea, one of Earth's most active volcanoes.

Stay Safe

Stay away from the affected regions until authorities allow people to return. When returning to homes and areas with lava, be careful. Don't walk on cooling lava. Avoid lava flows and stay away from responders working nearby.

DISASTROUS VOLCANOES

Volcanic eruptions on Earth have happened since prehistoric times. Scientists have only been able to study volcanoes that erupted before recorded history through rock evidence. Research indicates the supervolcano at Yellowstone in Wyoming erupted in a massive explosion about 640,000 years ago. This left behind the Yellowstone Caldera, a large volcanic crater.

The Yellowstone River flows through the northeastern part of the Yellowstone Caldera. The caldera measures 30 miles by 45 miles (48 kilometers by 72 kilometers).

Lava flows eventually filled in the Yellowstone Caldera. The last lava flow happened 70,000 years ago.

This volcano is still active. Earthquakes, ground changes and swelling, thermal springs, and geysers demonstrate its activity.

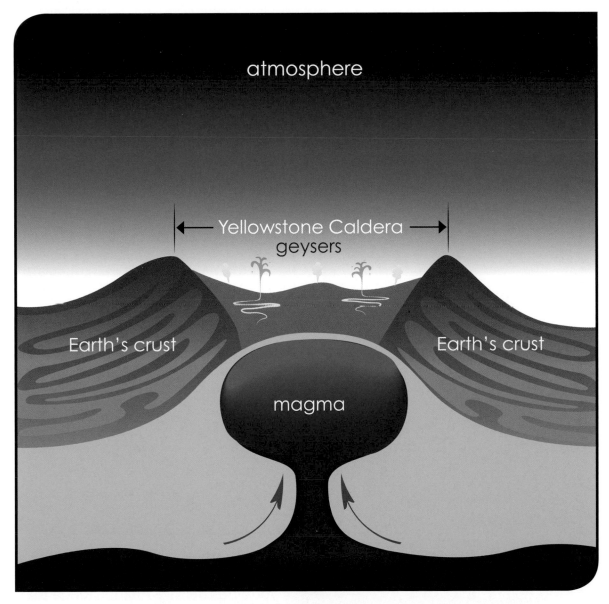

Magma near the surface of the Yellowstone Caldera is the cause of various geothermal activities, such as geysers, fumaroles, and hot springs. It heats the underground water and puts it under pressure so that it forces its way upward.

In 1783 the Laki volcano in Iceland erupted, lasting eight months. The particles in the air were so thick that most of the island's farm animals died from eating contaminated grass. Crop losses from acid rain caused a quarter of the people to die from starvation.

The Tambora volcano explosion in Indonesia in 1815 killed 10,000 people. Widespread ash moved over the area. More than 80,000 more people died from crop loss and starvation. The atmosphere changed, which cooled temperatures. After the eruption, 1816 became known as "The Year Without Summer."

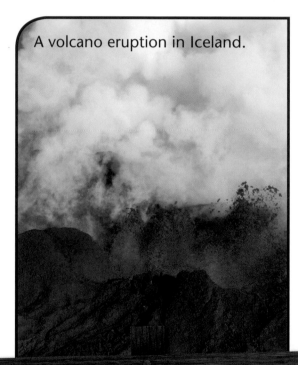

A volcano eruption in Iceland.

NORTH AMERICAN PLATE

EURASIAN PLATE

Mid-Atlantic Ridge

Krafla

ICELAND

Thingvellir
Reykjavik

Mid-Atlantic Ridge

ATLANTIC OCEAN

Did You Know?
Iceland is volcanically active because the island is over the Mid-Atlantic Ridge. This plate boundary is spreading and forming new crust. It also passes over a hot spot.

The North American plate and the Eurasian plates are spreading apart, forming the Mid-Atlantic Ridge that runs through Iceland. Magma wells up and fills this space, making it the source of the active volcanoes there.

Krakatoa, a volcanic island in Indonesia, erupted in a massive explosion in 1883. It changed the shape of the uninhabited island. The collapse caused a giant tsunami. Burning ash and the tsunami killed about 36,000 people in nearby towns and villages. The tsunami destroyed about 165 coastal towns.

Indonesia's location makes it prone to volcanoes. Indonesia lies on a subduction zone. The Indo-Australian plate is diving below the Eurasian plate. It has the largest number of volcanoes in the world with 147 volcanoes, 76 of them active.

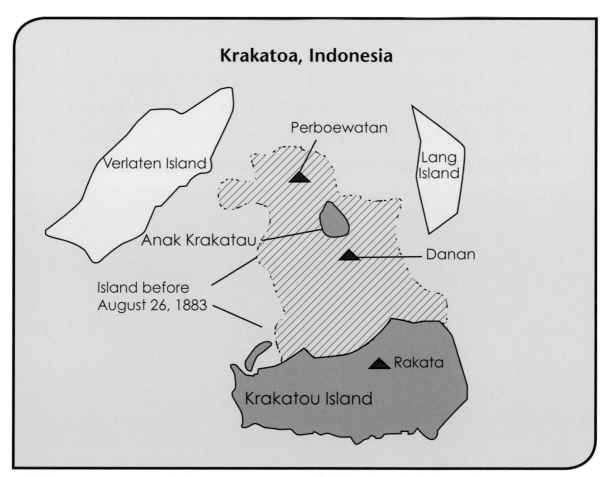

The explosion of Krakatoa blew away a big part of the island and the volcano's collapse dropped two of the mountains under the water in the resulting caldera.

June of 1912 brought a volcanic eruption at Novarupta, Alaska. It sent volumes of material in the air and lowered temperatures globally. The explosion brought ash flow that smoked for ten years.

Map showing Novarupta, Alaska

The largest eruption to affect a populated area happened on June 15, 1991. That's when Mt. Pinatubo in the Philippines erupted. Multiple earthquakes shook the area before the eruption. Afterward, avalanches of gas and hot ash, mudflows, and volcanic ash spread hundreds of miles wide.

More than 350 people died during the eruption of Mt. Pinatubo, most of them from collapsing roofs. The mud flows caused even more deaths. The eruption left more than 200,000 people homeless.

A blanket of ash and pumice covered the countryside. Ash reached the Indian Ocean. It circled the Earth two or three times. Most planes avoided the ash cloud. Some still flew through it and were damaged.

The emptied chamber lost so much material the top collapsed. Lava deposits filled the valleys and were so thick they held the heat for years.

The eruption still affects the region. Since then, monsoons and typhoons rain on the deposits and create lahars.

Haze and gases from the volcano caused a global temperature drop of one degree. Many towns were buried. Fields covered with lahar won't be usable for years.

People were warned ahead of time. This saved thousands of lives. More than ever is known about volcano eruptions. Predictions are still improving.

The hot lava falling on snow- and ice-covered volcanoes melts them and mixes with soil and volcanic material to form the mud in lahars.

Hot Fact
Lahar is a type of mudflow or debris flow made of volcanic material, rocky debris, and water.

PREDICTING VOLCANOES

Early warning signs of a coming volcano eruption help people prepare. They have time to leave the area.

Volcanologists study these warning signs. They learn the signals that mean an eruption is pending. Working around volcanoes can be a dangerous job. However, studying volcanoes and how they function provides information that helps scientists predict eruptions and hopefully save lives.

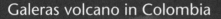

Galeras volcano in Colombia

Stanley Williams was studying the Galeras volcano in Colombia with a team of six co-workers. Suddenly the volcano that seemed dormant erupted without the usual warning signs. All the team but Williams died.

Caught in the eruption, hot gas and huge rocks exploded, breaking his legs, cracking his skull, and burning much of his body. Williams recovered and learned from his experience that volcanoes can be still before eruptions, too. He continues to study volcanoes and hopes to be able to warn people before an eruption.

Studying volcanoes involves a variety of jobs. Volcanologists travel to volcanoes to take samples during their field work. They measure the gases coming out. This signals changing volcano activity. They collect deposits left by the gases.

They take lava samples with a lava ladle. Field work also includes mapping mud and lava flows. They study exposed rock and the minerals in it. They date the rocks.

Boiling magma in a vent makes an enormous amount of noise. It rumbles, hisses, and roars as loud as a jet.

Volcanologists use many tools to study volcanoes. Instruments detect and record nearby earthquakes. They measure and record changes in the ground shape and in the movement of lava underground. They use video and still cameras, infrared cameras, satellites, and webcams to observe volcanoes. Everything volcanologists study helps them know more about volcanoes and find clues that a volcano may erupt.

Volcanologists don't spend all their time in the field, though. About a fifth of their work is on-site. Most of the work is done in the lab. There they analyze collected rock, mud, lava, and gas samples. They study old layers of lava to learn when the volcano may have erupted. They try to predict what it might do in the future.

Earthquakes signal possible eruptions of a volcano. Magma rising in the crust's cracks causes them. These earthquakes are measured and tracked. Volcano temperatures rise with increased activity.

Thermal imaging tools detect changes in heat around volcanoes. Gases, especially sulfur, means the volcano is closer to erupting. Chemical sensors monitor gas changes. This kind of monitoring is improving. The Mt. St. Helens eruption was predicted using these warning signs.

The Volcano Disaster Assistance Program (VDAP) monitors volcano activity and issues warnings. It provides help to people around the world.

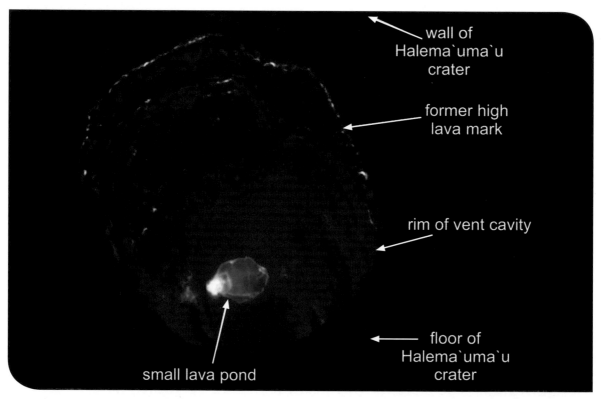

This thermal image, looking down into the Halema'uma'u crater vent in Hawaii, shows the heat levels of this pit crater in the Kilauea caldera. Deeper reds mean hotter temperatures.

These volcanologists take readings from delicate instruments to track the Merapi volcano in central Java, a province of Indonesia, which erupts every five to 10 years.

Be a Volcanologist

Becoming a volcanologist often begins by studying geology, the science of the Earth's rocks. You begin with science classes in high school. In college, you'll need to take many kinds of geology classes, including geology and physics, chemistry, and sediments.

You must learn to use the tools of a geologist. Not all colleges offer volcanology, but most that do are located closer to volcanic areas.

Many volcanologists teach college classes. Another job for a volcanologist is with the US Geological Survey (USGS), which operates three volcano observatories. States with volcanoes have their own geological surveys that offer more jobs.

Early gases from a volcano may help scientists predict an eruption in the future. Gases are collected from the vents and fumaroles, or openings around a volcano that release gases.

Volcano eruptions can't be prevented. Knowing an eruption will take place allows people to be prepared. Agencies and individuals can take the needed steps to be ready if a volcano happens.

Volcanoes can be beautiful but deadly. Understanding the Earth and its forces helps keep people safer.

One day volcano prediction will be better than ever. Reducing the loss of life in a disaster that can't be prevented is something volcanologists are always working to do.

WHEN DISASTER STRIKES

- Learn about the area where you live and find out the risks it holds for a volcano eruption.
- Make an emergency kit with first-aid supplies, food, water, and clothes to be prepared.
- Make a family plan about what to do and where you'll meet up.
- Organize a prevention campaign to help people know about volcanoes that might take place in your community.
- Help protect nature to reduce the risk of mudflows and landslides after a volcano.
- Help other kids if you evacuate to a shelter.
- Donate to emergency agencies such as the Red Cross.

GLOSSARY

basalt (buh-SAWLT): a dark, fine-grained igneous rock formed by cooling lava

caldera (kawl-DAIR-uh): a large, round opening at a mountaintop formed by an explosive volcano or when the side walls collapse and leave a depression

convection (kuhn-VEK-shuhn): heat that circulates through gases and liquids like molten rock

lahars (LA-harz): volcanic mudflows

magma (MAG-muh): molten rock inside the Earth

molten (MOHL-tuhn): melted under high heat to a liquid or liquid-like state

pyroclastic (pye-roh-KLAS-tik): a fast-moving rush of volcanic ash, rock, and gas from a volcanic eruption

rifts (RIFTS): cracks or fractures in hard materials from spreading

subduction (suhb-DUHK-shuhn): the place where two tectonic plates collide and one slides under the other

tectonic (tek-TAHN-ik): the shifting conditions in the Earth's crust that move its plates around

vents (VENTS): openings in the Earth's crust or volcanoes where magma moves up and out

volcanologists (valh-kuhn-AH-luh-jist): scientists who specializes in studying volcanoes

INDEX

SHOW WHAT YOU KNOW

1. Explain how the Earth's layers are involved in volcano eruptions.
2. Why would subduction plates cause more explosive volcanoes than those formed over a rift with spreading plates?
3. Describe the long-lasting effects of a volcanic eruption.
4. Why is the job of a volcanologist important?
5. Why is it important to study volcano eruptions from the past? Explain your reasons.

WEBSITES TO VISIT

www.unisdr.org/files/2114_VL108012.pdf
www.discoverykids.com/games/volcano-explorer
www.kids.nationalgeographic.com/explore/science/volcano

ABOUT THE AUTHOR

Shirley Duke has always been interested in how the Earth works and the forces that take place on it—especially volcanoes. Though there aren't any volcanoes in New Mexico right now, her home sits in a caldera of a long-dormant supervolcano. That explosion threw burning rock as far away as west Texas. She is a chidren's science writer and enjoys writing about science and nature.

Meet The Author!
www.meetREMauthors.com

www.rourkeeducationalmedia.com

PHOTO CREDITS: Cover © Dr. Richard Roscoe/Visuals Unlimited/Corbis; Title Page © Oystein Lund Andersen; page 4 © Vershinin-M; page 5 © snapgalleria; page 6 © graemes; page 7 © wildnerdpix; page 8 © U.S. Geological Survey/R.E. Wilcox/Wikipedia; page 9 © ttsz, U.S. Geological Survey/Lyn Topinka/Wikipedia, veni, F. Yoshikawa; page 10 © Gert Hochmuth, enote; page 11 © Wikipedia, beboy; page 12 © Milagli; page 13 © Yuri Arcurs; page 14, 35 © Jen Thomas; page 15 © designua; page 16 © theartist312; page 17, 40, 42 © U.S. Geological Survey/Wikipedia, Dr. Ajay Kumar Singh; page 18 © NASA; page 19, 34, 36, 37 © U.S. Geological Survey; page 20 © Simone Genovese; page 21,25 © andersen_oystein; page 22 © Sumos; page 23 © tupatu 76, edella; page 24 © Slim Sepp; page 26 © audioscience; page 27 © U.S. Geological Survey/CVO; page 28 © rszkutak; page 29 © kozmoat98; page 30 © Minko Chernev; page 31 © U.S. Geological Survey/AskHVO; page 32 © Ed Austin/Herb Jones; page 33 © Linar; page 34 © estivillml; page 36 © Frank Ramspott; page 38 © Atelopus; page 39 © Josecamilom/Wikipedia, Kim Kulish/Corbis; page 41 © TrueCapture; page 43 © Roger Ressmeyer/Corbis; page 44 © subemontes; page 45 © icholokov

Edited by: Keli Sipperley
Cover and interior design by: Jen Thomas

Library of Congress PCN Data

Volcanoes / Shirley Duke
(Devastating Disasters)
ISBN 978-1-63430-423-8 (hard cover)
ISBN 978-1-63430-523-5 (soft cover)
ISBN 978-1-63430-613-3 (e-Book)
Library of Congress Control Number: 2015931736

Also Available as:

ROURKE'S e-Books

Miranda

Miranda

by Tricia Tusa

Macmillan Publishing Company   New York

Collier Macmillan Publishers   London

Macmillan Publishing Company
866 Third Avenue, New York, N.Y. 10022
Collier Macmillan Canada, Inc.
Printed in the United States of America
10 9 8 7 6 5 4 3 2
Library of Congress Cataloging in Publication Data
Tusa, Tricia.
Miranda.
Summary: Miranda loves to play Bach, Haydn, and Mozart
on the piano, until the day she hears a one-man band
playing boogie-woogie.
1. Children's stories, American.   [1. Music—Fiction.
2. Piano music (Boogie woogie)—Fiction.   3. Pianists—
Fiction]   I. Title.
PZ7.T8825Mi   1985   [E]   84-21764
ISBN 0-02-789520-3

To my sister Sally,
whose playing boogie-woogie
made growing up a lot more fun.

This is Miranda.

Miranda loves to play the piano.

She plays stirring Bach, Haydn, and Mozart for Aunt Lorraine, Grandma Belle, Uncle Jay, and the rest of her relatives.

She plays a rousing school anthem for Mrs. Tillie Bean Quigley and the kids in her class.

And she plays scales so smoothly for her piano teacher,
Mr. Theodore.

Then one day, while walking home from school, Miranda hears a different kind of music. The beat is free and loose. Miranda runs down the street toward it.

Around the corner she comes, out of breath, and finds
a one-man band playing boogie-woogie. The old man plays with
such passion. The music fills the air with wild rhythm.

Miranda cannot help but move with it.

Thrilled, Miranda runs home and begins to play her own boogie-woogie! She plays it loud!

She plays it fast!

Miranda's hands slide and pound those keys. So do her head, elbows, knees, and feet.

Playing boogie-woogie makes Miranda very, very happy.

Miranda's playing boogie-woogie makes everyone else very, very unhappy.

"Why play such horrid noise!" cries Aunt Lorraine.

"You are wasting your talent, dear child," says Mr. Theodore.

"Stop that nonsense, Miranda!" shouts Mrs. Tillie Bean Quigley.

Miranda has had enough.

If she cannot play what she wants to play, then she simply will not play the piano. At all! Ever again!

And that is that!

Miranda shuts the piano lid.

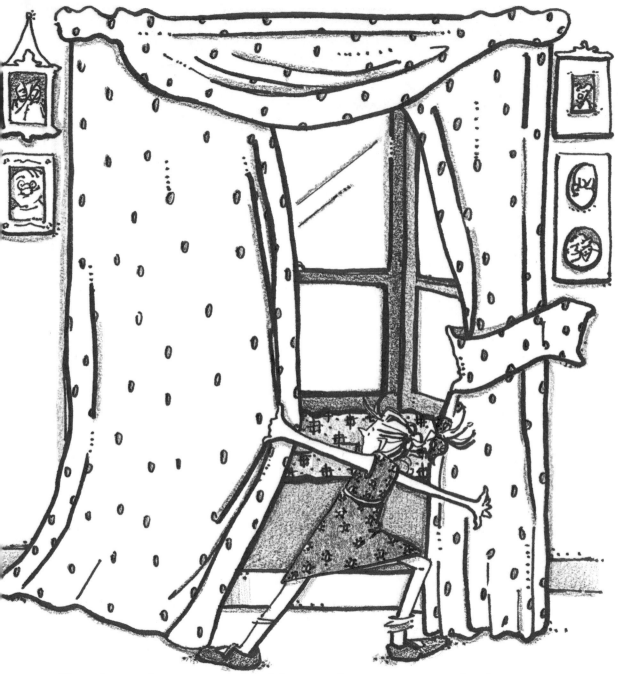

She closes the curtains and leaves the piano room, locking the door behind her.

Each day, a little more dust settles on the silent piano.

Each day, the house becomes quieter and quieter. Everyone tiptoes around and speaks in whispers.

No one has any appetite. There is not a smile in the place.

At school, the singing has stopped. The kids are miserable.

But the person who is suffering most is Miranda. Still, she stands her ground.

Finally, Miranda's mom shouts, "Enough of this awful silence! Any music is better than none! Miranda, you may play boogie-woogie!"

"Why can't I play both—classical and boogie-woogie?" Miranda replies.

The door to the piano room is opened. The curtains are drawn back.
The window is raised, and fresh air fills the room.
The dust is vacuumed off the piano.

And, once again, there is music! Miranda plays Mozart for
Aunt Lorraine and the gang. She plays the school anthem for
Mrs. Tillie Bean Quigley and her classmates. She plays her
scales over and over and over for Mr. Theodore.

But, for herself, Miranda plays
what now makes her happiest—boogie-woogie!